Life on Earth

This chart shows how the major animal groups connected. Using this you can see which groups are closely related to each other.

Shark

Sharks and rays

Sharks, rays, and related skates have flexible skeletons.

Snake

Lizard

Reptiles

Tortoise

Crocodiles, turtles and tortoises, lizards, and snakes are all types of reptile.

Birds

Owl

There are many types of bird, including penguins, owls, eagles, parrots, pelicans, songbirds, and woodpeckers.

Pelican

Mammals

Mammals feed their young on milk.

Salamander

Amphibians

Frog

The three groups of amphibians are frogs and toads, newts and salamanders, and snake-like caecilians (suh-si-li-uns).

Egg-laying mammals

Mammals that lay eggs are known as monotremes. They are the platypus and echidnas.

Kangaroo

Pouched mammals

These mammals, also called marsupials, keep their young in a pouch. This group includes kangaroos and opossums.

Bat

Whale

Cheetah

Placental mammals

This group contains anteaters, sloths, elephants, rabbits, rodents, bats, carnivores, hoofed mammals, whales, and primates – including humans!

Aardvark **Baboon**

Things to find out:

DK findout!
Animals

Author: Andrea Mills
Consultant: Dr Katie Parsons

Editor Olivia Stanford
Designer Lucy Sims
Project art editor Joanne Clark
Senior editor Gill Pitts
Managing editor Laura Gilbert
Managing art editor Diane Peyton Jones
Picture research Surya Sarangi
Pre-production producer Nadine King
Producer Srijana Gurung
Art director Martin Wilson
Publisher Sarah Larter
Publishing director Sophie Mitchell

Educational consultant Jacqueline Harris

First published in Great Britain in 2016 by
Dorling Kindersley Limited
80 Strand, London, WC2R 0RL

A CIP catalogue record for this book
is available from the British Library.
ISBN: 978-0-2412-5025-9

Printed and bound in China

A WORLD OF IDEAS:
SEE ALL THERE IS TO KNOW

www.dk.com

Contents

4 What is an animal?

6 Vertebrates

8 Mammals

10 Where mammals live

12 Birds

14 Reptiles

16 Amphibians

18 Fish

20 Invertebrates

22 Insects

24 What is a habitat?

Cat

Red fox

Giant rainforest mantis

Butterfly

26 Types of habitat

28 Deep and dark

30 Animal homes

32 Adaptation

34 Teeth

36 Food chains

38 Hunting

40 Defences

42 Camouflage

44 Attracting mates

46 Life cycle of a frog

48 Baby animals

50 Deadly animals

52 Meet the expert

54 Animals and us

56 Animal facts and figures

58 Top animals

60 Glossary

62 Index

64 Acknowledgements

Tarantula

Leopard tortoise

Goldfish

Gorilla

Parrot

Fire salamander

What is an animal?

Millions of different types of animal live on Earth. Each kind of animal is known as a species. Whether they are as tiny as an ant or as big as an elephant, all animals have a few things in common. For example, animals must eat other living things to survive, unlike plants, which get their energy from sunlight. Animals can also move from place to place, whereas plants cannot.

Breathing

All animals need oxygen to survive. They get it either by breathing air or by absorbing oxygen from water into their body. Dolphins live in water and breathe air through the blowhole on top of their head.

The toucan's long bill is useful for reaching food.

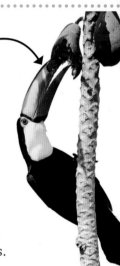

Feeding

Animals get their energy from food. Many are carnivores, which means they eat meat. Others are herbivores, which means they eat plants. Some animals, called omnivores, eat both animals and plants.

Powerful back legs allow grasshoppers to jump 20 times their own body length in a single leap.

Moving

Animals move around in a variety of ways, including hopping, jumping, running, crawling, slithering, flying, or swimming. Many animals use their legs to move, but others may use wings or fins.

Many animals are able to send messages to each other. This is called communication. They may use their voice, their face, and their body to communicate. Monkeys, like this mandrill, can scream a warning, while many birds have their own special song. Some animals, such as beetles, use chemical scents to send a message.

Communicating

Reproducing

Some female animals, such as seals, grow their young inside their bellies before giving birth. The babies may stay with their mother for a while to learn how to find food and avoid predators. Other animals, including birds and some reptiles and insects, lay eggs and protect them until the newborns hatch.

Mother seal

Baby seal

Reptiles use their tongues to smell their surroundings.

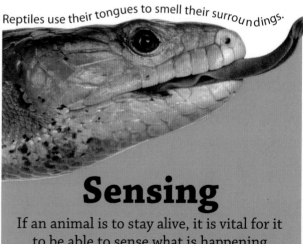

Sensing

If an animal is to stay alive, it is vital for it to be able to sense what is happening around it. The five major senses that animals use are sight, hearing, smell, taste, and touch. Some animals have extra senses and can detect electricity or even magnetism!

Vertebrates

Animals with backbones are called vertebrates. They have a bony skeleton under their skin and muscles, which provides a strong framework that supports their body and helps them move. They may look very different at first glance, but all vertebrate skeletons share some features, such as a skull to protect the brain.

Mammals have a large brain, which is protected by their hard skull.

The small bones of the backbone are called vertebrae.

Mammals

Only mammals have a lower jaw that is hinged directly to the skull. They also have specialized teeth, which means that they can bite, grip, tear, cut, chew, and grind their food. The planet's largest animals belong to this group, including whales, elephants, and tigers.

Fish

The first vertebrates were fish. Most fish, including carp, have a hard, bony skeleton. However, sharks and rays have a softer skeleton, which is made of a flexible material called cartilage.

Carp skeleton

The ribcage provides protective casing for the internal organs, such as the heart and lungs.

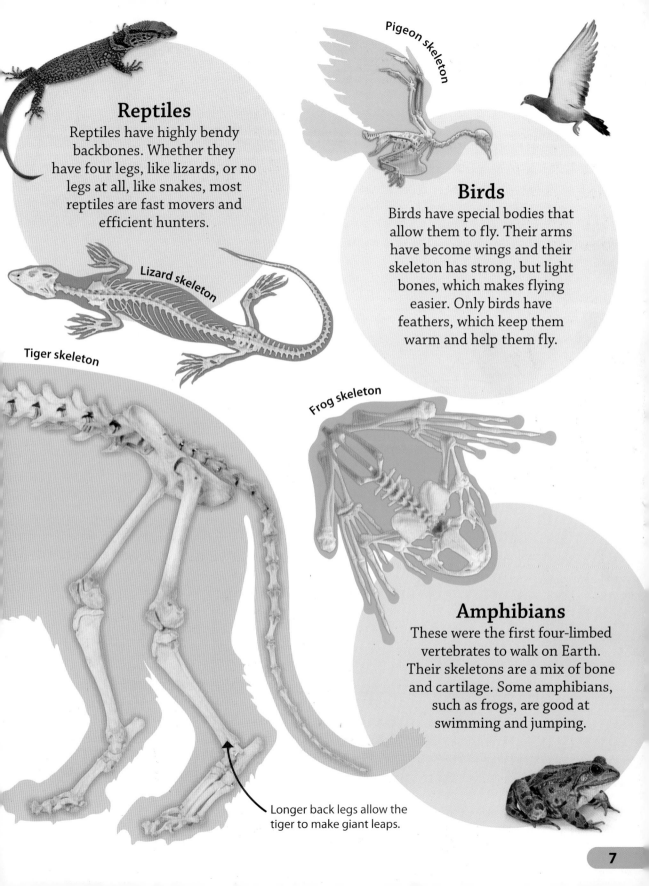

Reptiles

Reptiles have highly bendy backbones. Whether they have four legs, like lizards, or no legs at all, like snakes, most reptiles are fast movers and efficient hunters.

Pigeon skeleton

Birds

Birds have special bodies that allow them to fly. Their arms have become wings and their skeleton has strong, but light bones, which makes flying easier. Only birds have feathers, which keep them warm and help them fly.

Lizard skeleton

Tiger skeleton

Frog skeleton

Amphibians

These were the first four-limbed vertebrates to walk on Earth. Their skeletons are a mix of bone and cartilage. Some amphibians, such as frogs, are good at swimming and jumping.

Longer back legs allow the tiger to make giant leaps.

Mammals

From anteaters to zebras, and even humans like you, mammals come in all shapes and sizes. However, all mammals feed their young with milk. Most mammals give birth to live young, and almost all have hair on their body.

Warm blood
Mammals have a constant body temperature. They produce their own heat to keep warm or sweat to cool down. This means they can be active whether conditions are hot or cold.

Fur
Only mammals are covered in hair. Many hairs tightly packed together make fur. This protects the skin, and helps to keep the mammal warm and dry.

1   **Sea otters** have the thickest fur of all mammals. An adult may be covered in 800 million hairs.

2   **Female elephants** carry their baby for an incredible 22 months before they give birth.

3   **A common tenrec** holds the record for the most young born in one litter. She had 32 babies. Tenrecs are small mammals that live in Madagascar.

4   **Blue whale babies** are the largest on Earth. They weigh 2.5 tonnes (2.7 tons) when they are born.

5   **Hooded seal mothers** produce milk that is more than 60 per cent fat. That is richer than ice cream.

Milk

Female mammals produce milk to feed their young. The babies suckle from their mothers to drink the milk, which is packed with all the nutrients they need.

Feast for an African fawn
This young impala is drinking milk from its mother's udder while she keeps watch.

Types of mammal

There are more than 5,000 different types of mammal in the world today. They are divided into three groups, based on how their babies are born and raised.

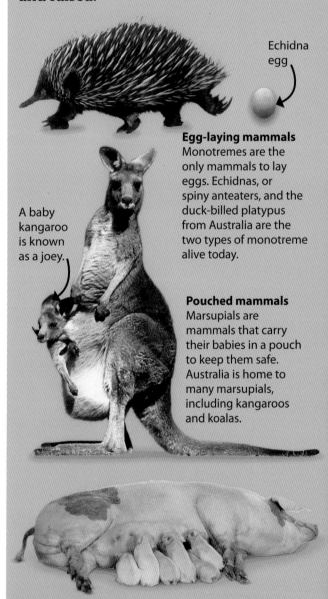

Echidna egg

Egg-laying mammals
Monotremes are the only mammals to lay eggs. Echidnas, or spiny anteaters, and the duck-billed platypus from Australia are the two types of monotreme alive today.

A baby kangaroo is known as a joey.

Pouched mammals
Marsupials are mammals that carry their babies in a pouch to keep them safe. Australia is home to many marsupials, including kangaroos and koalas.

Placental mammals
Placental mammals, such as pigs, give birth to babies that are more developed than marsupial babies. This is the largest group of mammals and includes humans.

Where mammals live

Mammals are most widespread and different on land, but they have also taken to the air and water. Bats have wings and are the only group of mammals that can fly. Aquatic mammals living in the sea have flexible flippers to help them swim.

Bears are the largest meat-eating animals (carnivores) living on land.

Squirrels use their bushy tail for balance when running along branches.

Camels store fat in their humps.

Giraffes have the longest neck of any living animal.

Gorillas are the largest of all the primates.

Anteaters lap up ants and termites through their tubelike snout.

Land

There are more types of mammal on land because there are so many different places where they can live. This might be a desert, a leafy forest, or even underground.

Sea

Mammals living in the sea can stay underwater for long periods of time. Their streamlined shape helps to make them very good at swimming.

Dolphins are fast swimmers and like to leap out of the water.

Manatees are slow-movers.

Elephants are the largest animals that live on land.

Fruit bats are also known as flying foxes. Some feed during the day.

Air

Most bats are nocturnal, which means they are active at night. They fly around, hunting for flying insects, such as moths, and other food.

Rhinoceroses have thick, tough skin.

Koalas are marsupials (pouched mammals), which spend most of their time in trees.

Zebras live in large herds on grassy plains.

Hares have large ears so they can listen out for predators.

Leopards are big cats that hunt at night.

Monkeys are very clever.

Armadillos have armour-like skin.

Hedgehogs have prickly spines for defence.

Moles dig tunnels with their spadelike hands.

Foxes are members of the dog family.

Whales are the largest animals alive today.

Seals dive deep looking for food.

Sea otters spend most of their time in water.

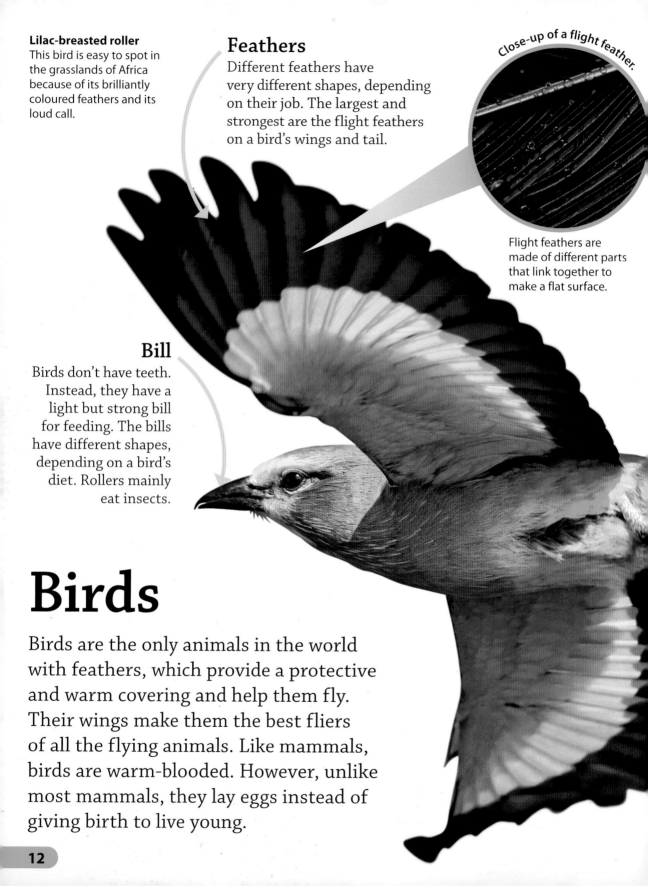

Lilac-breasted roller
This bird is easy to spot in the grasslands of Africa because of its brilliantly coloured feathers and its loud call.

Feathers

Different feathers have very different shapes, depending on their job. The largest and strongest are the flight feathers on a bird's wings and tail.

Close-up of a flight feather.

Flight feathers are made of different parts that link together to make a flat surface.

Bill

Birds don't have teeth. Instead, they have a light but strong bill for feeding. The bills have different shapes, depending on a bird's diet. Rollers mainly eat insects.

Birds

Birds are the only animals in the world with feathers, which provide a protective and warm covering and help them fly. Their wings make them the best fliers of all the flying animals. Like mammals, birds are warm-blooded. However, unlike most mammals, they lay eggs instead of giving birth to live young.

Eggs and nest

Most female birds make a nest, where they lay their eggs. The young grow inside, while the parents keep the eggs warm, taking it in turns to sit on them. When the time is right, the chicks peck their way out of the shell.

These eggs are ready to hatch.

Tail

The tail is used like a rudder to steer when flying, or for balance when the bird is perched on a branch or walking on the ground.

Feet

Birds are bipedal, which means they stand and walk on two feet. They have between two and four toes, which end in a sharp claw.

Wings

Instead of arms with hands, birds have wings. Birds fly either by flapping their wings or using them to glide in the air. A few birds can also hover.

Bird types

There are about 10,000 different types of bird living all over the world. They come in all shapes, sizes, and colours. Some are big, such as a heron, with a long bill and large wings. Others are small, but have a very loud song, like a blackbird.

Parrots are brightly coloured.

Kiwis cannot fly and only live in New Zealand.

Pigeons often live in cities.

Hawks have excellent eyesight.

Ducks have webbed feet for swimming.

Gulls feed in or near the sea.

Herons use their long legs to wade in water.

Blackbirds have a beautiful song.

Owls are active at night.

Penguins are good swimmers but cannot fly.

Reptiles

All reptiles have dry skin, which is protected by tough scales or horny plates. They are cold-blooded, which means their body temperature matches their surroundings. Most species of reptile eat other animals and lay eggs on land to produce young. Lizards are the most common type of reptile.

Scaly skin

The chameleon's skin changes colour depending on the light, temperature, and its mood. If it is angry or frightened, it may turn bright red, for example.

Other reptiles

Crocodiles and alligators walk on all four legs on land and use their long, powerful tails to swim in water. Snakes have no legs and move by flexing their long body. Tortoises and turtles are the only reptiles with a bony shell, which protects the body like a suit of armour.

Tail

As well as helping the chameleon to balance, its long prehensile tail is used to hold on to branches.

Crocodiles and alligators
The biggest reptiles are crocodiles and alligators. They hunt in lakes, rivers, and coastal areas. Their strong jaws and sharp teeth can kill prey as large as zebras.

Crocodiles have a more pointed snou than alligators.

Siamese crocodile

Panther chameleon

Chameleons are a special type of lizard with a tail that they use as a fifth limb when they are climbing in trees. Panther chameleons live in Madagascar and eat mostly insects.

Eye

The two eyes can move independently to look in different directions or they can both look at the same thing, such as prey.

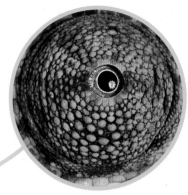

Tongue

The long, muscular tongue is flipped out to catch insects by trapping them on its sticky cup-like end.

Toes

The two sets of toes on each of the chameleon's feet give it a pincer-like grip as it moves along a branch.

The panther chameleon's tongue flips out and back with its prey in just 0.007 seconds!

Tortoises and turtles

Tortoises live on land and walk quite slowly on all four legs. Turtles spend most of their time in water and and have webbed feet or flippers for swimming.

A threatened cobra rears up and spreads its hood.

Snakes

All snakes catch live prey, which they swallow whole. Some snakes, such as cobras, kill their prey by injecting venom into them using their two needle-like teeth, called fangs.

King cobra

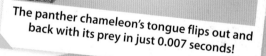

This tortoise has just hatched.

Leopard tortoise

Amphibians

Amphibians begin their life in water, where they breathe with gills. Most amphibians then grow a pair of lungs so that they can breathe when they are on land. They mostly have smooth skin, which must stay moist, so amphibians stay close to wet places when out of water.

Toads

Although they look like frogs, toads are larger and have shorter legs and drier skin. They spend more time on land than frogs.

Bumpy skin through which toads can breathe.

European green toad

Flattened tail for swimming.

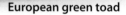
Common frog

Frogspawn consists of hundreds of black eggs, surrounded by protective jelly, laid in water by female frogs.

Frogs

Unlike other amphibians, frogs and toads have no tails as adults. They are the most common and so best-known of all amphibians. Frogs eat live prey, such as insects, catching them with their long, sticky tongue.

Webbed feet on the long back legs help frogs swim in water.

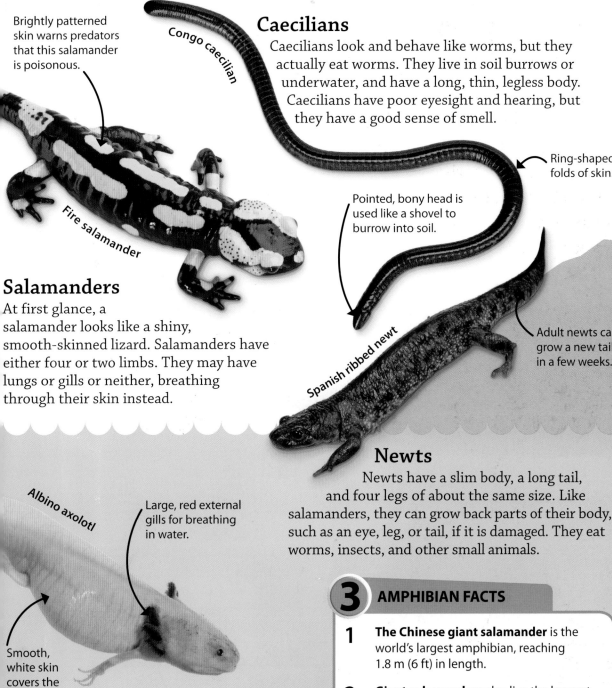

Brightly patterned skin warns predators that this salamander is poisonous.

Caecilians

Caecilians look and behave like worms, but they actually eat worms. They live in soil burrows or underwater, and have a long, thin, legless body. Caecilians have poor eyesight and hearing, but they have a good sense of smell.

Congo caecilian

Ring-shaped folds of skin.

Fire salamander

Pointed, bony head is used like a shovel to burrow into soil.

Salamanders

At first glance, a salamander looks like a shiny, smooth-skinned lizard. Salamanders have either four or two limbs. They may have lungs or gills or neither, breathing through their skin instead.

Spanish ribbed newt

Adult newts can grow a new tail in a few weeks.

Newts

Newts have a slim body, a long tail, and four legs of about the same size. Like salamanders, they can grow back parts of their body, such as an eye, leg, or tail, if it is damaged. They eat worms, insects, and other small animals.

Albino axolotl

Large, red external gills for breathing in water.

Smooth, white skin covers the plump body.

Axolotl

The axolotl is a unique type of salamander that spends all its life in water. It never develops the adult features that would allow it to move onto land, but it can still breed.

3 AMPHIBIAN FACTS

1 **The Chinese giant salamander** is the world's largest amphibian, reaching 1.8 m (6 ft) in length.

2 **Giant salamanders** also live the longest, reaching more than 50 years old.

3 **The fastest amphibian** is the Andean salamander, which has a top speed of 24 kph (15 mph).

Fish

There are about 32,000 types of fish in the world's oceans, lakes, and rivers. They are divided into three groups. Bony fish have a light but strong bone skeleton, and are by far the biggest group. Cartilaginous fish, which include sharks and rays, have a skeleton made of a bendy material called cartilage. Jawless fish only include lampreys.

Goldfish

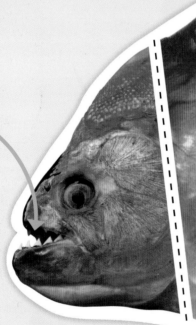

Gills
Instead of lungs, fish breathe with gills, which are positioned either side of the head. Water enters the mouth of the fish and leaves through the gills, which take oxygen from the water.

Piranha

Teeth
Fish have different types of teeth, depending on their diet. Meat-eating fish have pointed teeth to cut into prey. Piranhas have tiny teeth, but they are razor-sharp.

Eggs
Many female fish release thousands of eggs into the water, but some eggs are well-protected. A "mermaid's purse" is the casing that surrounds each egg of some sharks.

Mermaid's purse

Angelfish

Fins
Fish fins are found on different parts of the body. They are used to swim up or down, steer to one side, turn around, or act as brakes to stop the fish moving.

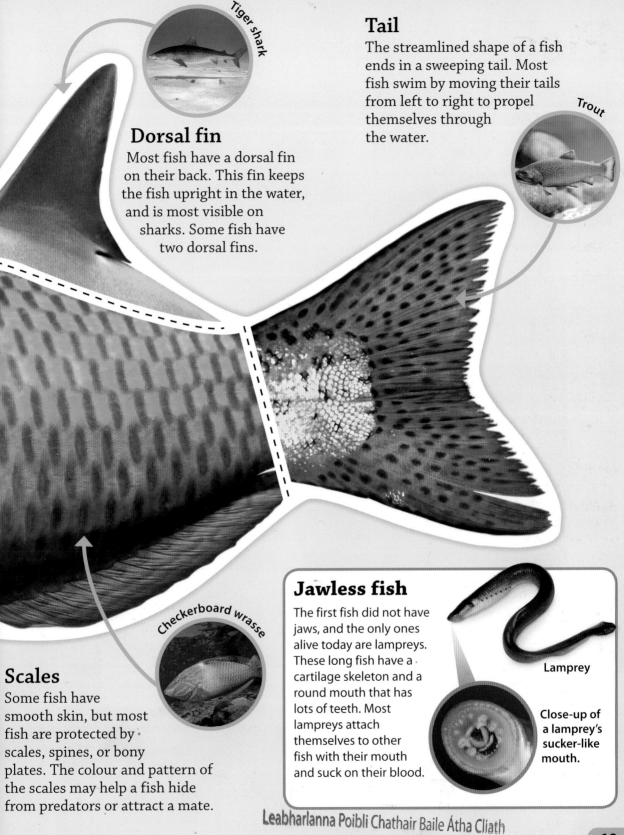

Dorsal fin

Most fish have a dorsal fin on their back. This fin keeps the fish upright in the water, and is most visible on sharks. Some fish have two dorsal fins.

Tiger shark

Tail

The streamlined shape of a fish ends in a sweeping tail. Most fish swim by moving their tails from left to right to propel themselves through the water.

Trout

Scales

Some fish have smooth skin, but most fish are protected by scales, spines, or bony plates. The colour and pattern of the scales may help a fish hide from predators or attract a mate.

Checkerboard wrasse

Jawless fish

The first fish did not have jaws, and the only ones alive today are lampreys. These long fish have a cartilage skeleton and a round mouth that has lots of teeth. Most lampreys attach themselves to other fish with their mouth and suck on their blood.

Lamprey

Close-up of a lamprey's sucker-like mouth.

Invertebrates

Animals with no backbone are called invertebrates. They are by far the largest group of animals, making up most of the life on Earth. Instead of a bony skeleton, their bodies use other substances for support or protection, such as fluid or shell.

Jellyfish are found in every ocean.

Moon jellyfish

Octopus

Vinegaroon

Tarantula

Spiders have eight legs and most have eight eyes.

Arachnids
All arachnids have a body that is divided into two main segments and four pairs of legs. Most spiders have venomous fangs, while scorpions come with a sting in their tail.

Whip spider

Snail

Molluscs
Molluscs have a wide range of body types, but they all have a soft body and many have a protective shell. Most molluscs are water-loving creatures, but quite a few are land-based, such as some slugs and snails.

Giant clam

Slug

Scorpion

Orb spider

Butterfly

Bug

Ants

Dragonfly

Spider crab

Wasp

Insects
These small creatures have three pairs of legs and a body divided into three parts. They use two feelers on their head to touch, smell, and taste. Many insects also have wings.

Mantis

Ladybird

Stick insect

Some insects, such as this wasp, may sting, and some have a strong bite.

Katydid

Fly

Beetle

Jellyfish

Jellyfish, anemones, and corals may look very different, but they are close relations. They all live in water and many of these simple animals have stinging tentacles for feeding and defence.

Anemone

Brain coral

97% of all animals are invertebrates!

3%

If these two pages represented every type of animal, all of the vertebrates would fit into this space! That is all fish, amphibians, reptiles, birds, and mammals!

Starfish and sea urchins

These animals live in the sea although they cannot swim. They have a distinctive symmetrical appearance, and spines and spikes for protection.

Sun star

Sea urchin

Lobster

Barrel sponge

Sponges cannot move around, unlike most other animals.

Sponges

Sponges are the simplest of all animals. They live in the sea, attached to rocks or coral reefs. The first sponges lived more than 600 million years ago.

Starfish usually have five arms, but some have up to 40.

Starfish

Crustaceans

These tough-bodied invertebrates are at home in water. They have jointed legs and a body divided into segments. Large crustaceans, such as crabs and lobsters, use their claws to capture and kill prey.

Earthworms eat things such as rotting leaves that are found in soil.

Stove-pipe sponge

Leech

Earthworm

Worms

Worms have long, soft, segmented bodies. They breathe through their skin, so they have to keep it damp if they live on land. Bristles on their body help them to move around.

Crabs have 10 legs, but the first pair are used as claws.

Ragworm

21

Insects

There are more insects on Earth than any other group of animals. Over one million different species have been found so far, but there may be as many as 10 million! Their small size and their ability to fly means that insects are found in a wide range of habitats around the world.

Insect body parts

The body of an insect is divided into three parts. The head houses the brain, and supports the eyes, feelers, and mouthparts. All insects have six legs on the thorax and many have wings. The abdomen contains the organs for digestion and reproduction.

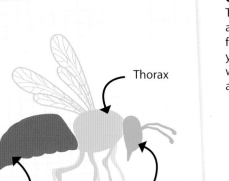

Thorax

Head

Abdomen

Common wasp
This insect buzzes around hunting for food. Its black and yellow stripes are a warning that it has a painful sting.

Stinger can be used again and again.

Useful insects

Although some insects are pests, they are important to a lot of living things, particularly flowering plants. They are the main source of food for many animals, and humans find some insects useful, too.

Silkworm cocoon

Silk moths
Silkworms spin a silk cocoon around themselves when they are ready to change into the adult moth. People have used this silk to make cloth for more than 5,000 years.

Adult silk moth

Wings

Wasps have two pairs of transparent wings, which they beat at high speed to fly fast, turn, and hover.

Feelers

All insects have two feelers, or antennae, which they use to touch, smell, and taste their surroundings.

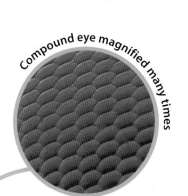

Compound eye magnified many times

Eyes

Their two large compound eyes, which have thousands of tiny lenses, mean that insects are excellent at spotting something moving.

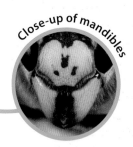

Close-up of mandibles

Mouthparts

Most insects have biting jaws, or mandibles. Behind the jaws are straw-like tubes, which they use to suck up liquid food, such as nectar.

Legs

Insects have three pairs of jointed legs, which they use for walking and gripping. Some insects are also good jumpers.

Bumblebee drinking nectar.

Bees
Bees are important because they pollinate flowers, including some human food crops. Honeybees produce sweet honey from nectar.

Edible insects
Insects are high in protein, and 27 per cent of people in the world eat them. Crunchy crickets are a popular snack.

Dried crickets

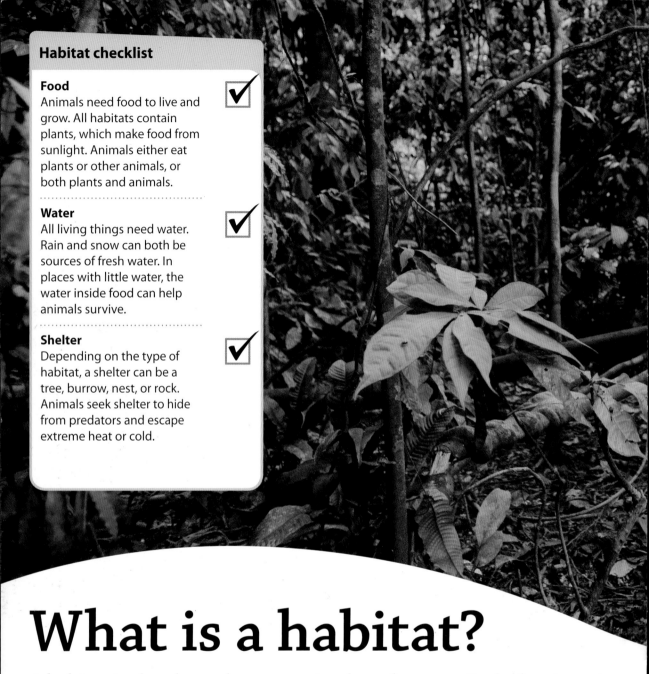

What is a habitat?

A habitat is the place where an animal or plant can find what it needs to live, including food, water, and shelter. There are all sorts of different habitats around the world. One of the most important habitats is tropical rainforest, because so many different types of animal and plant live in it. Tropical rainforest is mostly found in South America, Africa, and Southeast Asia.

Rainforest dwellers

Rainforests are bursting with life. The warm, wet weather is perfect for plants, which means plenty of food for animals. Birds nest in the treetops, monkeys swing from the branches, and big predators, such as leopards, stalk the forest floor.

Giant rainforest mantis
One of Australia's largest mantises, this fierce insect has a big appetite. It feasts on other insects such as butterflies and dragonflies.

Monkey-tailed skink
A skilled climber, the monkey-tailed skink lives in the Solomon Islands, near Australia. It feeds on fruit and leaves, using its flexible tail to cling to branches.

Types of habitat

From baking hot deserts to snowcapped mountains, the world is made up of many different habitats. Animals live in the habitat where they are best-suited to the temperature, weather, and food that is found there. Many different types of animal and plant live side by side in most habitats.

Microhabitats

A microhabitat is a habitat on a miniature scale. It can be as tiny as the space under a stone. The smallest difference in temperature or the amount of moisture will make a microhabitat more attractive to one type of animal than another. A seaside rock pool is an example of a microhabitat and is home to lots of living things.

Rock pool

Mountain
The snowy peaks and lower slopes of cold mountains are home to a few tough animals. Any land that measures more than 600 m (2,000 ft) in height is called a mountain.

Forest
More animals live in forests than any other habitat on land. The three main forest types are steamy rainforests, cooler temperate rainforests, and cold coniferous forests.

Grassland
Hot grasslands that have a rainy season and a dry season are called tropical grasslands. Temperate grasslands have some rain all year, and both hot and cold seasons.

Desert
One of the world's most difficult habitats to live in is desert, because less than 25 cm (10 in) of rain falls in a year. Temperatures are high in the day and very cold at night.

Polar
The polar regions of the Arctic and Antarctica are frozen worlds of floating ice caps and howling winds. These extreme places are empty lands with few plants or animals.

Ocean
The world's oceans make up two-thirds of our planet's surface. Scientists think that this huge habitat is home to millions of different types of animal that have yet to be discovered.

Golden eagle
These birds of prey nest high in the mountains. Their superb eyesight helps them spot prey, such as a mountain hare, from 3 km (2 miles) away.

Brown bear
Trees provide leafy cover for brown bears as they search for food. Their thick fur keeps them warm in the cold winters of coniferous forests.

Wildebeest
The tropical grassland of Africa is called savanna. Wildebeest eat the grass, but they must move during the dry season to find enough to eat.

Side-winding adder
This snake's colours merge with the desert sand to hide it from predators and prey. It gets water from the lizards that it eats.

Arctic hare
A fluffy white coat helps the Arctic hare blend into the icy landscape. In severe storms, these hares dig snow shelters to keep warm.

Tropical fish
Many different types of colourful tropical fish live in warm seas, often around coral reefs. The reefs offer a place to live, hide, and search for food.

Deep and dark

The deepest depths of the oceans are more than 1,000 m (3,280 ft) under the surface. This extreme habitat has huge challenges for the animals that live there. Fish and other marine life live with permanent darkness, bitter cold, very little food, and crushing pressure from the huge amount of water above. Scientists can only see these animals by using a special vehicle called a submersible.

Fangtooths live at depths of 5,000 m (16,400 ft).

Some comb jellies produce their own light.

Fangtooth

Many deep-sea fish like this fangtooth have jaws that can stretch and sharp teeth ready to trap any food they find. At 15–18 cm (6–7 in) long, the fangtooth has the biggest teeth compared to its size of any fish.

Comb jelly

Comb jellies are invertebrates that have eight rows of thousands of tiny hairs called combs on the surface of their body. They move around by beating the combs.

Extreme survivor

There is nothing tougher than a tardigrade. Also called "water bears", these tiny animals, which are usually less than 1 mm ($\frac{1}{25}$ in) long, can live in the deepest oceans. They can also survive dry conditions, and being frozen or boiled. Tardigrades can even live in space!

The big fins look like the ears of an elephant.

Like a lure on a fishing rod, this glowing fin attracts prey.

Dumbo octopus

These octopuses live deeper in the ocean than any other type of octopus. They hover along the sea bed at depths of up to 4,000 m (13,100 ft) in search of prey.

Anglerfish

Instead of swimming around, the anglerfish lures its prey within reach. It has a massive mouth that can swallow large prey whole.

Sea cucumber

These marine animals are called sea cucumbers because they are a similar shape, and sometimes colour, to the vegetable. Their closest relatives are starfish and sea urchins.

Sea cucumbers look for scraps on the sea floor.

Animal homes

There's no place like home, and animals are amazing architects. They are creative builders, making all kinds of different houses in which to live or have their young. Safety, shelter, and warmth are all important features of a home, whether high up in the treetops or down on the ground. Nature provides many materials, such as grass, branches, and mud, for animals to build their houses.

Den

Foxes and bears build dens. A female polar bear digs out a snowy den in the Arctic, where she gives birth in winter. She rears her cubs for three months, until the cubs are ready for the world outside.

Web

Some animals make their own materials. Spiders have a special silk-spinning organ in the rear of their body called a spinneret. They weave silk into intricate webs, which are used to trap prey.

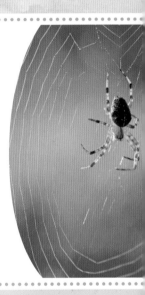

Lodge

Busy beavers choose watery locations to build a lodge because they are excellent swimmers. Mud and branches are used to make a safe structure with entrances underwater to prevent predators entering.

A beaver family inside their lodge.

Sett

Badgers dig deep to construct networks of underground chambers and tunnels. These shy creatures emerge from their sett at night to feed.

Drey

What looks like a tangle of sticks in a tree may be a squirrel's home. Dreys are built with leaves, twigs, and moss. Winter dreys are bigger and thicker to keep the squirrels extra warm.

Nest

Not only birds make nests. Wasps build nests using paper they make by chewing on wood and plants. These strong structures are ideal places to lay eggs and rear young.

Mound

Tiny termites use teamwork to build mighty mounds, reaching 10 m (33 ft) high! They are made from termite saliva and dung mixed with soil. Holes in the walls let air enter and cool the mound.

Termites working inside the mound.

Shell

Imagine carrying your home on your back! Hermit crabs use empty seashells to live inside. When the shell gets too small for the growing crab, it finds a bigger one.

Adaptation

If an animal is well-suited to its habitat we say it has an adaptation. The better-adapted it is, the more likely it is to survive. For example, a penguin's thick feathers are a perfect adaptation for keeping it warm in the snow, but would make it far too hot in a desert.

In the desert

Sandy deserts are hot places without much water. Some animals, like camels, have become well-matched for this environment. They can survive without water for days, have a store of fat in their hump for energy, and long eyelashes to keep out the sand.

A beak is perfect for catching fish, but there aren't any in the desert.

Dark feathers absorb heat, which make the penguin too hot in the desert.

Dense feathers cover a thick layer of fat, for warmth. The penguin would overheat on the hot sand.

Small wings are used for swimming, but there is nowhere to take a dip here!

Dromedary camel

Emperor penguin
This bird has many things that help it to keep warm in icy Antarctica. If you put it in the desert it would quickly overheat.

Thorny devil
This spiky lizard lives in deserts in Australia. Unlike feathers or hair, scales lose heat quickly so if it found itself in the snow this lizard would freeze.

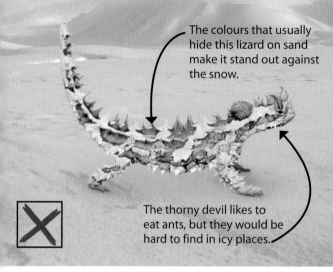

The colours that usually hide this lizard on sand make it stand out against the snow.

The thorny devil likes to eat ants, but they would be hard to find in icy places.

In the snow
It's a challenge to stay warm in snowy places. The Arctic fox has a thick coat of hair to keep it cosy. Its fur is grey in the summer, but in winter its fur is white to blend in with the snow. This helps it to sneak up on prey.

Arctic fox

Under the sea
Many types of animal are adapted to living in the salty sea. The blacktip reef shark has a streamlined body to help it glide through the water and, like all sharks, it has gills that allow it to breathe underwater.

Males "quack" to attract mates, but they wouldn't be heard underwater.

Green treefrog
Frogs need fresh water to live. If a green treefrog fell into the sea, the high amount of salt would be toxic to it and it would die.

Strong back legs are useful for swimming, but this frog prefers to live on land.

Blacktip reef shark

Teeth

A quick trip to a dentist would reveal a lot about what animals eat for dinner. Most animals have no teeth at all. Some animals, such as reptiles, have only one type of tooth. Mammals have three types of teeth. Incisors at the front of the mouth cut into food, and canine teeth in the corners grab and tear. Molars at the back of the mouth chew and grind food.

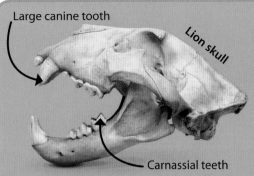

Large canine tooth

Lion skull

Carnassial teeth

Carnivore

Animals that eat only meat are called carnivores. Meat-eating mammals include lions, tigers, and wolves. They have long, pointed canines, which they use to stab and grip prey. Their sharp carnassial teeth work like shears to slice meat into chunks for swallowing.

! WOW!

Snails have the **most teeth** of any animal. They have **thousands of tiny teeth** lined up in rows.

Lion
Their teeth may be made for killing, but male lions let the females do most of the hunting. When the lionesses catch a meal, such as a zebra, the male lion always eats first.

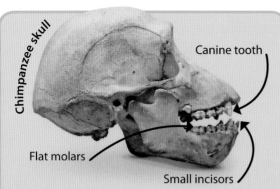

Canine tooth

Flat molars

Small incisors

Omnivore

Animals that have a mixed diet of meat, fruit, and plants are called omnivores. Their incisors, canines, and molars give them a mix of sharp and flat teeth for eating different types of food. Raccoons, hedgehogs, chimpanzees, and humans are examples of omnivores.

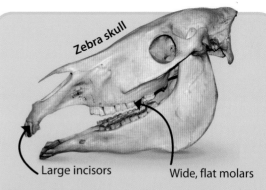

Large incisors

Wide, flat molars

Herbivore

Plant-eating animals, such as sheep, cows, and zebras, are called herbivores. They use their incisors to snip off mouthfuls of grass and leaves. Their strong molar teeth have a large flat surface and they chew the tough food for a long time before swallowing.

Chimpanzee
Humans and chimpanzees are related. They both have 32 teeth, but chimpanzees have larger canine teeth than humans.

Zebra
Zebras live on the huge grassy plains of Africa. They move around to find the best grass to eat.

Food chains

No living thing can survive without food. A food chain shows how a specific set of plants and animals are linked together by who eats what. Each arrow in a food chain means "is eaten by". The chain ends when it reaches an animal that has no natural predators. If one link is removed, the chain will break.

Leaves

Producer

Almost every food chain begins with a plant. These plants are called "producers" because they create, or produce, their own food by combining the energy in sunlight with water and air.

Complete the food chains

Do you know which of the animals below fits into the two incomplete food chains?

1

Coyote
This wild member of the dog family lives in America, feasting on animals, insects, and fruit.

2

Killer whale
The biggest member of the dolphin family swims in the oceans, hunting marine life and seabirds.

3
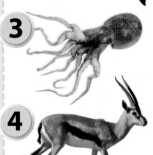
Octopus
This unusual animal uses its six arms and two legs to search the sea for fish and crabs.

4

Gazelle
At home in Africa and Asia, this antelope leaps around the plains, feeding on grass and shrubs.

A
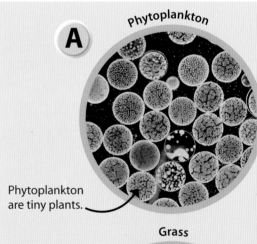
Phytoplankton

Phytoplankton are tiny plants.

B

Grass

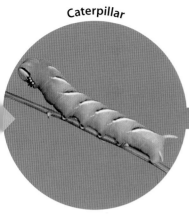

Caterpillar

Robin

Owl

Primary consumer

Herbivores feed on plants. They are the first, or primary, animals in the food chain and they eat, or consume, producers. A caterpillar is a primary consumer because it eats leaves.

Secondary consumer

Animals that eat herbivores are secondary consumers. They can be carnivores, which eat other animals, or omnivores, which eat animals and plants. A robin is a secondary consumer.

Tertiary consumer

Tertiary consumers are mainly carnivores. They feed on secondary consumers. This owl is the end of this food chain, as it is not eaten by any other animal, but other food chains can be shorter or longer.

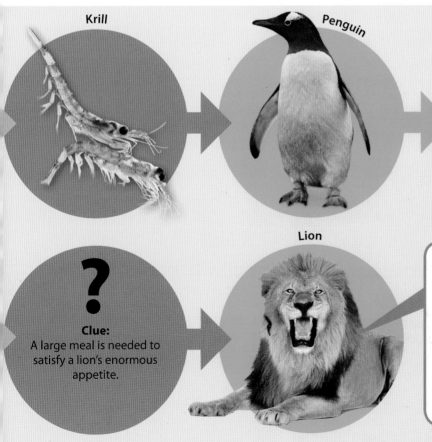

Krill

Penguin

?

Clue:
Only a large marine animal could manage to eat a penguin.

?

Clue:
A large meal is needed to satisfy a lion's enormous appetite.

Lion

Apex predator

An animal at the very top of a food chain is called an apex predator. These animals are not hunted by anything. An example is the African lion, which kills its prey but has no natural predators to worry about.

Stalk

A red fox has such good hearing it can detect rodents, such as lemmings and mice, moving in their tunnels 1 m (3 ft) below the snow. It stalks its prey silently, ready to pounce in an instant.

Pounce

The fox dives headfirst into the snow, using its sharp claws to dig deeper for the prey.

The fox's ears locate even the faintest sounds of movement.

The back legs launch the fox into the air.

Front legs are raised, ready to pounce.

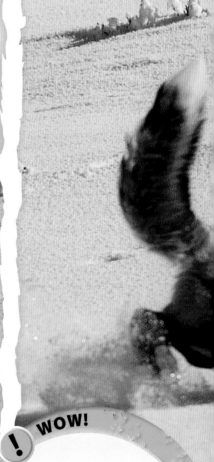

Hunting

Meat-eating animals must find food to survive. They have to detect, stalk, and catch prey time after time. Hunting techniques are learned at a young age from parents and during play. Solo predators, like foxes, use skill and speed to catch prey, while pack animals, such as wolves, work as a team to catch larger animals.

! WOW!

A **great white shark can smell blood** in water up to **5 km (3 miles) away.**

Farming and herding

Leafcutter ants are the farmers of the insect world, working as a team to grow fungus, which they eat. They carry leaves to their nest for the fungus to grow on. Other ants keep herds of small plant-eating insects called aphids, and feed on the honeydew they give out.

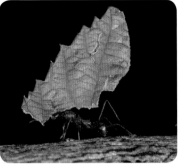

Ant carrying a leaf in its jaws.

Ant feeding on honeydew.

The fox's body lands directly on top of the target.

Its head is completely buried in the snow.

Success!

The fox finds its meal, trapping the rodent in its strong jaws before pulling it to the surface to eat.

The rodent has no chance of escaping the fox's jaws.

Defences

Survival in the animal kingdom is not easy. With predators a constant threat, animals have adopted all kinds of different defences to protect themselves. For some, the best form of defence is attack. These animals bite or kick, or rely on poison. Others choose to lie low, hiding from danger or playing dead.

SPIKES

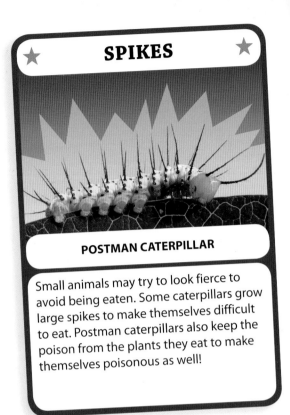

POSTMAN CATERPILLAR

Small animals may try to look fierce to avoid being eaten. Some caterpillars grow large spikes to make themselves difficult to eat. Postman caterpillars also keep the poison from the plants they eat to make themselves poisonous as well!

STARTLE

PRAYING MANTIS

This praying mantis uses a combination of defences. Usually, it is hard to spot because it looks like a dried-up leaf. However, if a predator gets too close, the dead leaf mantis opens up its arms and wings, flashing bright colours that surprise the attacker and scare it away.

PLAY DEAD

OPOSSUM

Some animals fake their own deaths to avoid being eaten. If a Virginia opossum sees a predator, it curls up and stops moving. This state can last for hours, making it look like it is dead. It even releases a rotting smell, so predators leave it alone and search for fresh prey instead.

ARMOUR

ARMADILLO

For slow-moving animals, body armour can be a life-saver. A hard shell or tough skin can be a real challenge for a predator. The three-banded armadillo is covered in overlapping bony plates. When it rolls into a ball there is no way for a hungry hunter to get to its head or soft belly.

! WOW!

Lizards like the **tokay gecko** have got a clever trick to escape danger. If a **predator grabs its tail, it comes off** and the gecko can **run away!**

SMELL

SKUNK

Bad smells can keep predators away, especially when the whiff is like rotten eggs! Skunks are too slow to escape at speed, so they spray a foul-smelling liquid from their rear end. This eye-watering scent is so powerful it can be detected 1.6 km (1 mile) away.

SHOAL

SNAPPERS

A small fish travelling alone is an easy target for predators. Many fish species, such as these black spot snappers, stick together in shoals of hundreds. Each individual fish gets lost in the crowd, so it is much harder for a victim to be singled out by a predator.

Camouflage

Animals use colours, patterns, or even shapes to blend in with their surroundings. This is called camouflage, and some animals are masters of deception. Danger is part of life in the animal kingdom, but camouflage is a great survival technique to avoid hungry predators or to sneak up on prey.

Spot the moth!

Can you find the moth hiding on this tree bark?

Hide and seek

There are many ways in which animals hide from each other. Some copy an object, such as a flower, or change colour completely, while other animals group together to have safety in numbers.

Leaf-tailed gecko

Lookalike
Is it a twig? Is it a leaf? No! It's a leaf-tailed gecko from Madagascar! Some animals mimic (copy) an object in their surroundings, such as a dead leaf, so a predator won't recognize them.

Herd of zebras

Double vision
Stripes offer camouflage in the grasslands as patterns blend in with foliage. Faced with a herd of zebras, a predator will struggle to choose a single target in the sea of stripes.

Disguised moth
It is easy to miss a peppered moth, but look again. When this moth rests flat against a tree, its patterned wings merge perfectly with the bark.

Can you see the crab spider catching the hoverfly?

Colour change
Some crab spiders can change colour from white to yellow to match the flowers they live on. Then they can creep up on their insect prey, such as this hoverfly.

Attracting mates

It is often the males of the animal kingdom that have to win over a mate. By showing off their good looks or their best dance routine, they demonstrate to females that they are healthy and strong. They are keen to prove themselves as the best fathers to their future offspring.

A large number of brightly coloured eyespots catches the female's attention.

Showing off

The peacock's mating ritual is a stunning show in which he struts around with pretty patterned feathers fanned out behind him. The female peahen looks at his tail display to decide whether he is a suitable mate.

The peahen has dull brown feathers to help her hide from predators.

There can be up to 150 feathers in a male peacock's tail.

Animal attraction

Males don't stop at visual displays. Some go to much greater lengths to find a mate, such as giving presents or fighting each other to see who is stronger.

This male nursery web spider is giving a gift of an insect wrapped in silk to persuade the female to take him as her mate.

Male bowerbirds create a beautiful display to attract the females, decorating their "bowers" with their favourite colourful items.

Male giraffes fight by slamming their necks against each other. Whoever comes out on top in the contest shows their strength and wins the female.

Life cycle of a frog

The changes to an animal's body from the beginning of its life until its death is called the life cycle. Most amphibians, such as frogs, start life looking very different to their parents. The incredible process by which a tiny tadpole changes shape as it grows older and finally reaches its adult form is called metamorphosis.

RIBBIT! RIBBIT!

An adult male common frog sits near a pond and calls out loudly to attract the attention of a female frog.

The male frog and the female frog meet in the water and he holds onto her. When the female lays her eggs, the male fertilizes them.

Between one and three weeks later, the eggs hatch into tiny, legless tadpoles. They have gills for breathing in the water.

The female frog lays hundreds of eggs, called frogspawn, in the water. Each egg is protected by a thick layer of jelly.

Mouth

Gills for breathing

Tail for swimming

YUM! DELICIOUS!

The front legs develop next, and the body changes to look more like that of a frog. The tadpole is now big enough to eat small animals, such as water fleas.

Tail starts to shrink

Each tadpole feeds on algae and other tiny plants. It grows bigger, and its back legs start to form after five weeks or so.

Water fleas

After 14 weeks, the tadpole has changed into a miniature frog. Instead of gills, the froglet now has lungs so it can breathe air. The froglet can swim in water, hop on land, and catch insects, such as small flies.

HOME SWEET HOME!

In spring, the adult frog returns to the pond where it was born. It is ready to find a mate, and the life cycle begins for a new generation.

1 This chick starts life with downy feathers.

2 This baby must eat a lot to prepare for its transformation.

3 This swimming nymph has not yet developed its wings.

A

Dragonfly
Newborn animals may live in different habitats to their parents. Dragonfly babies, or nymphs, live underwater, but fly in the open air as adults.

B

Brush-tailed possum
This Australian marsupial has a big, bushy tail and is covered in thick fur. Females carry one baby, called a joey, inside a protective pouch.

C

Leaf monkey
Leaf monkeys live in Asia's rainforests. The adults have dark grey fur, but the babies are brightly coloured so their mothers can find them.

Baby animals

In the animal kingdom, there is not always a family resemblance between babies and their parents. Newborns may have different colours, textures, and patterns, or even take another shape before they mature into adulthood. Try this quiz to see if you can identify who are the parents of these baby animals.

Spots and stripes provide camouflage for this baby.

5

4

6

This tiny baby is born without hair and with its eyes closed.

This newborn has orange fur for its first six months.

D

E

F

Budgerigar

These colourful birds are the smallest members of the parrot family. Baby birds are born covered in fluffy down before growing full feathers.

Tapir

Related to rhinoceroses and horses, tapirs begin life with protective camouflage. Adults lose this pattern as predators are less of a threat.

Butterfly

Some insects, like butterflies, change into adults through an amazing process called metamorphosis. Their body changes shape completely.

Seeing double

Sometimes there is no mistaking who is the mother or father. These newborns look like miniature versions of their parents.

A baby lizard catches a ride on its mother's back.

Baby guinea pigs stay close to their mother.

This baby seahorse is a tiny version of its father.

Deadly animals

Approach this lot at your peril! Not all animals are furry and friendly. Some specialize in producing poisons or venom. Poison is deadly if touched, but venom must be injected to have its toxic effect. Poisons can put off potential predators, but venomous fangs can be used to kill prey.

Actual size

Box jellyfish

This scary stinger of the seas can kill in an instant. Each long venomous tentacle contains 5,000 stinging cells with the power to kill fish and other marine life, and even people, so don't swim too close to one!

This jellyfish has 200 different chemicals in its venom.

Inland taipan

Nicknamed "the fierce snake", Australia's inland taipan has the most toxic venom of any snake in the world. Rats are its main prey and they are bitten several times before the snake swallows them whole.

One bite from an inland taipan contains enough venom to kill 100 people!

Despite its nickname, this snake is actually very shy and is rarely seen.

Golden poison dart frog

This frog has poisonous skin, and is the most poisonous animal in the world. A single golden poison dart frog could kill 10 people, but it is only found in the Colombian rainforest.

Brazilian wandering spider

The Brazilian wandering spider is a fast mover. In towns and cities, it hides during the day in dark places, such as a log pile or an old box, and will give a potentially fatal bite if it is accidentally disturbed.

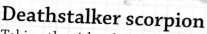

MOST POISONOUS!

Faking it

Bright colours often mean an animal is deadly. Venomous coral snakes are so feared that harmless milk snakes have changed over time to look like them. The milk snake's skin now looks so similar to the coral snake's that predators avoid them.

IMPOSTER!

Harmless milk snake

Venomous coral snake

Deathstalker scorpion

Taking the title of most deadly animal is the deathstalker scorpion. Although its venom is less toxic than others, this desert scorpion kills the most people because it is aggressive, striking at night, and stinging on sight.

Meet the expert

We meet Professor David Macdonald, director of the Wildlife Conservation Research Unit (WildCRU) at the University of Oxford, UK. He and his team study lots of animals around the world, but have a special interest in lions.

Q: We know it is something to do with animals, but what is your actual job?

A: Wildlife conservation means trying to help animals that are in danger of dying out in the wild. This may be because too many are being hunted by people, or for other reasons. For example, there may be a problem with people becoming angry because wild animals, such as leopards or tigers, are killing and eating their cattle. So I will try to find a way to help the animals and people to live alongside each other.

Q: What made you decide to try to help to save lions?

A: I chose lions because their numbers are falling fast. There are just over 20,000 lions left in Africa today, compared to 100,000 only 50 years ago.

Radio tracking
One way of keeping track of a group of lions is to place a radio transmitter around the neck of one of them.

This lioness has been given a drug to make her sleep while a new radio collar is fitted around her neck.

A receiver is used to pick up the signals from the lioness's radio collar.

Q: What is a usual work day for you?

A: One day I might be out in the field searching for wild animals or signs of their activities. The next day might be spent talking to local villagers or working with people to come up with a law that will protect the animals. I also spend a lot of time looking at the information we have collected on the animals.

Q: Do you need special equipment to study wild animals?

A: Wildlife conservation needs a mix of traditional skills and modern technology. Sometimes we can find an animal by looking for its footprints, but we also use satellites in space to follow the movements of lions across hundreds of kilometres.

Q: Is it dangerous tracking lions?

A: Working with big, fierce animals like lions is less dangerous than much of city life, so long as you understand their behaviour and treat them with care.

Q: What are the biggest problems for lions and what can you do to help them?

A: Losing places where they can live and hunt in safety, and upsetting local people even though they don't mean to. We help by showing villagers how they can keep their cattle safe from lions, and we use satellite tracking to warn them when the lions are moving towards their farms.

Releasing a young badger back into its home wood.

Studying badgers
Professor Macdonald also studies badgers in the UK. They are caught, measured, and weighed every four months.

Q: What are the best and worst things about your job?

A: Many wild animals are in danger and often the problems are difficult to solve. However, the best thing about my work is improving the lives of both the animals and the people living close to them. I also get to work in beautiful places with amazing animals.

Animals and us

The ancestors of today's domesticated animals once ran wild. Over thousands of years, humans have taken different types of wild animal and changed the way they look and behave. Animals provide us with food, clothing, transport, and labour, and we have welcomed them into our homes as pets.

Large, floppy ears on a small head look attractive to people.

Short legs and a long body mean this small dog could squeeze into a badger's home.

Dachshunds can be long-haired, short-haired, or wire-haired, and their fur can be different colours.

FACT FILE

Dogs

There are about 350 breeds of dog. Today, most dogs are kept as pets, but they were originally bred to perform different tasks. Dachshunds were once used to track badgers underground.

Dachshund

» **Length:** 32–60 cm (12–24 in)

» **Weight:** 4–12 kg (9–26 lb)

» **Diet:** Dried dog food, meat, bones, biscuits

» **Habitat:** Homes

» **Life expectancy:** 12–15 years

Useful animals

Some domestic animals, such as dogs and cats, live in our homes and are treated like members of the family. Other animals are kept for more practical reasons.

Chickens are kept for their meat and the eggs that the hens lay. Their feathers may be used to fill pillows.

Cats are good at catching pests like rats and mice as well as being a furry friend.

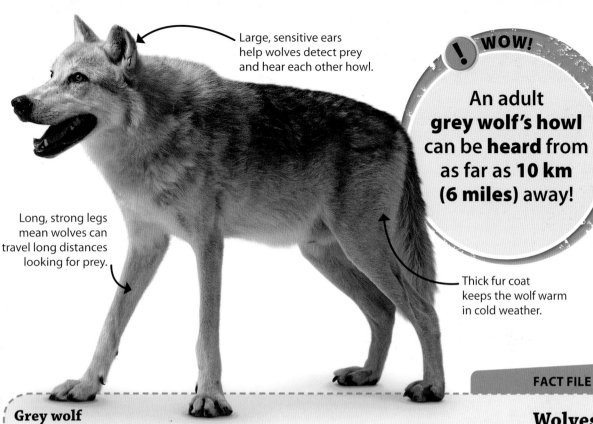

Large, sensitive ears help wolves detect prey and hear each other howl.

Long, strong legs mean wolves can travel long distances looking for prey.

An adult **grey wolf's howl** can be **heard** from as far as **10 km (6 miles)** away!

Thick fur coat keeps the wolf warm in cold weather.

FACT FILE

Grey wolf
- » **Length:** 1–1.5 m (3–5 ft)
- » **Weight:** 16–60 kg (35–130 lb)
- » **Diet:** Elk, deer, reindeer, rabbits, squirrels, fish
- » **Habitat:** Forests, mountains, northern polar regions
- » **Life expectancy:** 6–13 years

Wolves

The grey wolf is the ancestor of all the different types of pet dog. It lives in packs of about eight adults, led by a top male and female pair. By hunting as a team, wolves can catch very large animals.

Llamas are hardy pack animals, helping people transport heavy loads. Their wool is used to make warm clothing.

One cow can produce gallons of milk every day. Cows are also kept for their meat, called beef, and their skin is used to make leather.

Animal facts and figures

Animals are a fascinating group. Here are some weird and wonderful facts you might not know about them!

Giant pandas spend up to **16 hours a day** eating bamboo.

A vampire bat can drink 50 per cent of its body weight in blood in just 30 minutes.

South America's basilisk lizard **can run on water.**

47,000,000

red crabs walk from the forests of Christmas Island in the Indian Ocean down to the sea every year. Their journey takes the crabs about a week.

An Arabian oryx

can smell rain falling up to 80 km (50 miles) away.

Hummingbirds are the only bird that can **fly backwards!**

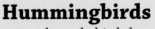

Hummingbirds flap their wings about 60 times per second when hovering.

In 1960, British chimpanzee expert **Jane Goodall** discovered that **chimps can make and use tools.**

Chimp using a rock to crack a nut.

18

is the number of hours that a koala sleeps every day. The rest of their time is spent eating and resting.

A mole can tunnel through 100 m (330 ft) of soil in a day.

3

is the number of hearts that an octopus has.

Top animals

Animals are amazing! From the fastest, loudest, strongest, and tallest to the smallest animal of all, every record-breaking animal is a winner. How do you think you would compare to the animals shown here?

Fastest on land

The cheetah can reach a speed of 115 kph (70 mph) in just 3 seconds. The fastest a human has ever run is 45 kph (28 mph).

Strongest animal

The dung beetle can pull a weight that is 1,141 times heavier than its own body. That is the equivalent of a human pulling six buses at once.

Heaviest spider

A female Goliath birdeater weighs about 170 g (6 oz), which is roughly the same weight as a medium-sized apple. The male is much smaller.

Tallest animal

The giraffe is the world's tallest living animal, stretching up to 6 m (20 ft) thanks to its long legs and extremely long neck.

Longest-living animal

The giant barrel sponge can live for up to 2,300 years. That is more than 10 times as long as the bowhead whale, which is the longest-lived mammal.

Shortest life span

Adult mayflies live for only one day. They do not feed, and they die after they have found a mate and the female has laid her eggs.

Deepest-diving bird

The emperor penguin can dive as deep as 565 m (1,850 ft). It stays underwater for up to 22 minutes as it hunts for prey.

The sailfish can swim at a speed of 110 kph (68 mph) in short bursts. That means it can swim 10 times its body length in 1 second.

The snow leopard can leap as far as 15 m (50 ft) when chasing after prey such as wild goats. That is about 15 times its body length.

Cuvier's beaked whale can dive to depths of almost 3 km (1.9 miles). One whale stayed underwater for a record 2 hours and 18 minutes.

The bee hummingbird is 5 cm (2 in) long, and weighs just 1.6 g (just over $^1/_{20}$ oz). It lays eggs that are smaller than a pea.

Fairyflies are too tiny to see. The smallest fairyfly is 0.16 mm ($^3/_{500}$ in) long, and would easily fit inside the full stop at the end of this sentence.

The pistol shrimp snaps its claws to make a bubble of air in water. When it bursts, the 218 decibel sound produced is louder than a gunshot.

Kitti's hog-nosed bat weighs as little as 1.5 g ($^1/_{20}$ oz) and is 3 cm (just over 1 in) long. It is also called the bumblebee bat.

The blue whale is 33 m (108 ft) long and weighs 150 tonnes (165 tons). It is roughly as big as a jumbo jet, and its heart is the size of a small car.

The Arctic tern flies 71,000 km (44,000 miles) between the Arctic and Antarctica and back every year, for up to 30 years.

Glossary

Here are the meanings of some words that are useful for you to know when learning about animals.

adaptation Way in which an animal or plant becomes better-suited to its habitat. For example, a penguin's thick feathers keep it warm in icy places

amphibians Cold-blooded vertebrates that start life in water before moving between land and water when fully grown

ancestor Animal or plant to which a more recent animal or plant is related

aquatic Something that lives in water

armour Naturally hard body covering that provides protection for an animal

arthropod Group of invertebrates with a tough outer skeleton and a body divided into segments

birds Warm-blooded vertebrates with feathers that can usually fly

camouflage Colours or patterns on an animal's skin, fur, or feathers that help it merge with the environment

carnivore Animal that eats only meat

cartilage A tough but flexible material found in animals and that makes up the skeletons of sharks

A chameleon is cold-blooded.

cold-blooded Animal with a body temperature that goes up and down to match the surrounding air or water temperature

conservation Trying to stop an animal or plant from becoming extinct

coral Hard outer skeleton of tiny sea animals, which can build up into widespread reefs in warm seas

courtship Special types of animal behaviour, which are attempts to attract a mate

domesticated Animals kept as pets or on farms. They may have been raised in a house or on a farm

environment Surroundings in which an animal or plant lives

extinction When all of a particular animal or plant species die out and there are none left in the world

gills Organs of fish and some amphibians that allow them to breathe underwater

habitat Natural home environment of an animal or plant

A frog is an amphibian.

herbivore Animal that eats only plant matter

invertebrate Animal without a backbone

lungs Breathing organs found inside the body of vertebrates

mammals Warm-blooded vertebrates that have skin covered in hair and feed their young milk

marine Describes animals and plants that live in the sea

metamorphosis Process by which some animals transform themselves into a different form from youth to adulthood. For example, a tadpole becomes a frog

microhabitat Small habitat, such as the underside of a leaf

mimic Animal that copies the appearance or behaviour of another

nocturnal Animals that are active at night, when they hunt or feed

nutrients Different types of food that animals need to survive

omnivore Animal that eats both plant matter and meat

plumage Word used to describe all of the feathers of a bird

poison Harmful substance released by an animal or plant that may be deadly if touched or eaten

predator Animal that hunts other living animals for food

prehensile Grasping body part, such as the tail of a chameleon

prey Animal that is hunted for food

primate Group of mammals, which includes monkeys

reproduce To have young

reptiles Cold-blooded vertebrates with scaly skin that reproduce by laying eggs, such as snakes, lizards, and crocodiles

scavenger Animal that feeds on the leftover meat of another animal that has already died, whether by a predator attack or natural causes

species Specific types of animals or plants with shared features that can mate and produce young together

symmetrical Shape with two perfectly matching parts

temperate Area or climate with mild temperatures

toxic Substance that is dangerous, such as poison

tropical Area or climate with hot temperatures and high rainfall

vegetation Plant life found in a particular habitat

venom Harmful substance released by an animal or plant that may be deadly if injected into the skin, by a sting or fangs

vertebrate Animal with a backbone

warm-blooded Animal that keeps a constant body temperature

Index

A

adaptation 32–33
alligators 14
amphibians 7, 16–17
anglerfish 29
anteaters 10
ants 39
apex predators 37
Arabian oryxes 57
arachnids 20
Arctic hares 27
Arctic terns 59
armadillos 11, 41
axolotls 16–17

B

badgers 31, 53
bats 11, 56, 59
bears 10, 27, 30
beavers 30
bees 23
bills 12
birds 7, 12–13, 25
blackbirds 13
body armour 41
bowerbirds 45
breathing 4
budgerigars 49
butterflies 49

C

caecilians 17
camels 10, 32
camouflage 42–43
carnivores 34, 37, 38–39
caterpillars 37, 40
cats 54
chameleons, panther 14–15

cheetahs 58
chickens 54
chimpanzees 35, 57
cold-blooded animals 14
comb jellies 28
communication 5
compound eyes 23
conservation 52–53
consumers 37
coral reefs 27
cows 55
coyotes 36
crabs 21, 31, 56
crickets 23
crocodiles 14
crustaceans 21

D

defence 40–43
dogs 54
dolphins 10
domestic animals 54–55
dragonflies 48
ducks 13
dung beetles 58

E

eagles 27, 38
eggs 9, 13, 14, 16, 18, 46
elephants 9, 11
eyes 15, 23

F

fairyflies 59
fangtooths 28
feathers 12, 32, 44–45
feeding 4
feelers 20, 22–23

fins 18, 19, 29
fish 6, 18–19, 27, 28–29, 41
food 24
food chains 36–37
forest habitats 24–27
foxes 11, 30, 33, 38–39
frogs 16, 33, 46–47, 50–51
fur 8, 33

G

gazelles 36
geckos 41, 43
gills 16–17, 18, 46–47
giraffes 10, 45, 58
gorillas 10
guinea pigs 49
gulls 13

H

habitats 10–11, 24–29, 32
hawks 13
hedgehogs 11
herbivores 35, 37
herons 13
homes 30–31
hummingbirds 57, 59
hunting 38–39, 55

I

insects 20, 22–23
invertebrates 20–21

J

jawless fish 19
jellyfish 21, 50

K

kiwis 13
koalas 11, 57
krill 37

L

lampreys 19
leopards 11, 25
life cycles 46–47
lions 34, 37, 52–53
lizards 6, 14–15, 41, 49,
    56
llamas 55

M

mammals 6, 8–11, 34
manatees 10
mantises 25, 40
marsupials 9
mates, attracting 44–45
mayflies 58
metamorphosis 46
microhabitats 27
milk 8, 9
moles 11, 57
molluscs 20
monkeys 11, 25, 48
monotremes 9
moths 42–43
movement 4

N

nests 13, 31
newts 17

O

octopuses 29, 36, 57
omnivores 35, 37
opossums 40
orangutans 25
owls 13, 37
oxygen 4

P

packs 38, 55
pandas, giant 56
parrots 13
peacocks 44–45
penguins 13, 32, 37, 58
phytoplankton 36
pigeons 13
placental mammals 9
possums, brush-tailed 48
producers 36

R

rabbits 11, 38
reproduction 5
reptiles 7, 14–15
rhinoceroses 11
rock pools 26
rollers, lilac-breasted 12–13

S

sailfish 59
salamanders 17
scales 14, 19, 33
scorpions 20, 51
sea cucumbers 29
sea otters 9, 11
sea urchins 21
seahorses 49
seals 9, 11
senses 5
sharks 19, 33
shells 20, 31
shelter 24, 30
shoals 41
shrimps, pistol 59
silkworms 22
skeletons 6–7
skin 14, 16
skinks, monkey-tailed 25
skunks 41
smell 5, 41

T

snails 20, 34
snakes 15, 27, 50–51
snow leopards 59
spiders 30, 43, 45, 51, 58
spiny devils 33
sponges 21, 58
squirrels 10, 31
starfish 21

T

tadpoles 46–47
tails 13, 14, 19
tapirs 49
tardigrades 29
teeth 6, 18, 34–35
tenrecs, common 9
termites 31
toads 16
tortoises 15
turtles 15

V

venom 50–51
vertebrates 6–7

W

warm-blooded animals 8
wasps 22–23, 31
water 24
webs 30
whales 9, 10–11, 36, 59
wildebeest 27
wings 6, 12–13, 20, 22–23
wolves 38, 55
worms 21

Y

young 8, 9, 13, 14, 16, 48–49

Z

zebras 11, 35, 43

Acknowledgements

The publisher would like to thank the following people for their assistance: Ruth O'Rourke and Kathleen Teece for editorial assistance, Alexandra Beeden for proofreading, Helen Peters for compiling the index, Neeraj Bhatia for cutouts, and Gary Ombler for photography. The publishers would also like to thank Professor David Macdonald and his team at the Wildlife Conservation Research Unit (WildCRU) for the "Meet the expert interview", and Martin French of Bugz UK and Mark Amey of Amey Zoo for animals and handling.

The publisher would like to thank the following for their kind permission to reproduce their photographs:

(Key: a-above; b-below/bottom; c-centre; f-far; l-left; r-right; t-top)

3 **Corbis:** Don Farrall / Ocean (cb). **Dorling Kindersley:** Natural History Museum, London (tr). 4 **Alamy Images:** Nature Picture Library (clb); Malcolm Schuyl; Rolf Nussbaumer Photography (cr). 5 **Alamy Images:** Image Source (t). **Getty Images:** Tom Brakefield / Photodisc (bl). 6 **Dorling Kindersley:** Blackpool Zoo (clb). 8-9 **FLPA:** Frans Lanting (c). 9 **Dorling Kindersley:** Booth Museum of Natural History, Brighton (fcra); Jerry Young (ca). 10-11 **Alamy Images:** WaterFrame (b). 10 **Alamy Images:** Life on White (crb). **Dreamstime.com:** Greg Amptman (br). **Fotolia:** Eric Isselee (ca). 11 **Corbis:** image100 (crb). **Dorling Kindersley:** Jerry Young (c). **Fotolia:** Eric Isselee (fcr). 12-13 **Alamy Images:** Johan Swanepoel (c). 12 **Alamy Images:** Daniel Kulinski (tr). 13 **Dorling Kindersley:** Cotswold Wildlife Park & Gardens, Oxfordshire, UK (br); Neil Fletcher (ca); Liberty's Owl, Raptor and Reptile Centre, Hampshire, UK (fcr); E. J. Peiker (cb). 16 **Alamy Images:** Life On White (clb). 18 **Alamy Images:** Arterra Picture Library (bl). **Corbis:** (crb); Pete Oxford / Minden Pictures (c); Don Farrall / Ocean (cr); Norbert Probst / Imagebroker (bc). **Dreamstime.com:** Dean Bertoncelj (cl); Tdargon (tc). 18-19 **Corbis:** Eiko Jones (c). 19 **Alamy Images:** Lamprey (crb); Masa Ushioda (tc). **Corbis:** Jelger Herder / Buiten-beeld / Minden Pictures (br); Jeff Hornbaker / Water Rights (c); Norbert Probst / Imagebroker (cb). **Dreamstime.com:** Lukas Blazek (cra). 20 **Dorling Kindersley:** Forrest L. Mitchell / James Laswel (fcrb); Liberty's Owl, Raptor and Reptile Centre, Hampshire, UK (fclb); Natural History Museum, London (clb). **Dreamstime.com:** Johan007 (crb). 21 **Alamy Images:** Linda Pitkin / Nature Picture Library (tc). **Dorling Kindersley:** Natural History Museum, London (cla); Linda Pitkin (cra). **Dreamstime.com:** Stubblefieldphoto (crb). 22 **Dorling Kindersley:** Natural History Museum, London (br). 22-23 **Alamy Images:** OJO Images Ltd. 23 **Corbis:** Steve Gschmeissner / Science Photo Library (tr); Albert de Wilde / Buiten-beeld / Minden Pictures (cr). 24-25 **naturepl.com:** Anup

Shah. 27 **Corbis:** Jim Brandenburg / Minden Pictures (cb); John Hyde / Design Pics (tc); W. Rolfes (ca/Brown Bear); Valentin Wolf / Imagebroker (ca); Michael & Patricia Fogden (c); Stuart Westmorland / Image Source (b). 28-29 **Alamy Images:** PF-(usna1) (b). **Corbis:** Nature Picture Library (cb); Norbert Wu / Minden Pictures (t). 28 **naturepl.com:** David Shale (crb). 29 **naturepl.com:** David Shale (cla). **Science Photo Library:** Eye Of Science (cra). 30 **FLPA:** Ingo Arndt / Minden Pictures (bc); Matthias Breiter (tr); Imagebroker / Gerken & Ernst (cr). **Getty Images:** Russell Burden (bl). 31 **FLPA:** Ingo Arndt / Minden Pictures (crb); Roger Wilmshurst (tl). 32 **Corbis:** Tariq_M_1 / Room The Agency (bl). **Getty Images:** David Tipling / Digital Vision (cr). 33 **Alamy Images:** ArteSub (bl). **Corbis:** Roberta Olenick / All Canada Photos (cra). **Getty Images:** Paul Oomen (tl). 34 **Dreamstime.com:** Mike Carlson (br). 35 **Alamy Images:** Sabena Jane Blackbird (tr). **Corbis:** Cyril Ruoso / Minden Pictures (bl). **Dorling Kindersley:** The Natural History Museum, London (tl). **Dreamstime.com:** Duncan Noakes (br). 36 **Alamy Images:** Blickwinkel / Mcphoto / Bio (crb). **Dorling Kindersley:** Greg and Yvonne Dean (bl); Andy and Gill Swash (cl). **Dreamstime.com:** Musat Christian (fclb). 37 **Corbis:** F. Lukasseck / Masterfile (cb). **Dreamstime.com:** Isselee (bc). 38 **Alamy Images:** David Hosking (l). 38-39 **Alamy Images:** David Hosking. 39 **Alamy Images:** FLPA (ca); David Hosking (r). 40 **123RF.com:** Marion Wear (cb). **Corbis:** Joe McDonald (crb). 41 **123RF.com:** cbpix (crb). **Alamy Images:** Redmond Durrell (tl, cla). 42-43 **Corbis:** Ingo Arndt / Minden Pictures. 43 **Corbis:** Frans Lanting / Mint Images (cr); Michael Quinton / Minden Pictures (bc). **FLPA:** Nicolas Cegalerba / Biosphoto (ca). 44-45 **Alamy Images:** Aditya "Dicky" Singh. 45 **Alamy Images:** Blickwinkel / Lohmann (br); Photoshot (cra); Dave Watts (cr). 48 **FLPA:** Bernd Rohrschneider (c). **Getty Images:** Herman du Plessis (tl). **naturepl.com:** Fiona Rogers (cr). 49 **Alamy Images:** John Cancalosi (tc); Jamie Craggs / Papilio (br). **Dorling Kindersley:** Cotswold Wildlife Park (c, tl); Natural History Museum, London (cr). **Dreamstime.com:** Bidouze Stéphane (tl). **FLPA:** Mitsuaki Iwago / Minden Pictures (bc). **Getty Images:** James Gerholdt (bc/Gecko). 50 **Alamy Images:** Kelvin Aitken / Visual&Written SL (cl). **Dreamstime.com:**

Ben Mcleish (bc). 51 **Alamy Images:** Barry Turne (tr). **Corbis:** Imagemore Co., Ltd / Imagemore Co Ltd. (cb). **Dorling Kindersley:** Twan Leenders (br). 52 **(c) David Macdonald** (www.wildcru.org); WildCru (all images). 53 **Andrew Harrington:** (tr 54 **Alamy Images:** Hollie Crabtree (br). 55 **Alam Images:** Moodboard (br). **Dorling Kindersley:** Jerry Young (tl). **Dreamstime.com:** Eric Isselée (bl). 56-57 **Corbis:** Poelking, F. 56 **123RF.com:** czalewski (crb). **Corbis:** Ingo Arndt / Minden Pictures (bc); Bence Mate / Visuals Unlimited (clb) Nature Picture Library (br). **Dorling Kindersley:** Jerry Young (cla). 57 **123RF.com:** szefei (fclb). **Corbis:** Hans Overduin / NiS / Minden Pictures (ca); Christian Zappel / imagebroker (cl); Cyril Ruoso / Minden Pictures (cr); Reinhard, H. (cb). **naturepl.com:** Aflo (bl). 58 **Corbis:** Cisca Castelijns / NiS / Minden Pictures (bc); Suzi Eszterhas / Minden Pictures (tr); Rolf Nussbaumer / Nature Picture Library (cl); Pete Oxford / Minden Pictures (c); Erich Schmidt / Imagebroker (cr); Michele Westmorland (bl). **Getty Images:** Frank Krahmer / Photographer's Choice (br). 59 **Alamy Images:** Kevin Elsby (cl); Nature Picture Library (tr). **Corbis:** (tl); Tim Fitzharris / Minden Pictures (tc); Fred Bavendam / Minden Pictures (cr); Flip Nicklin / Minden Pictures (bc). **FLPA:** Photo Researchers (bl). **Science Photo Library:** Dr. Harold Rose (c)

Cover images: _Front:_ **Dorling Kindersley:** Natural History Museum, London cra; **Dreamstime.com:** Musat Christian fcr; **Fotolia:** Jan Will fcra; **Getty Images:** Aditya Singh c; **naturepl.com:** Mark Bowler tr; _Back:_ **Dorling Kindersley**: Forrest L. Mitchell / James Laswel clb Natural History Museum, London tc; Front Flap: Dorling Kindersley: E. J. Peiker br/ (Inside); Fotolia: Eric Isselee bc, clb/ (inside); Back Flap: Dorling Kindersley: Natural History Museum, London clb, Gary Ombler / The University of Aberdeen tl/ (front); **NASA:** JSC cb/ (front)

All other images © Dorling Kindersley
For further information see:
www.dkimages.com

My Findout facts:

Amphibians

Key features
- Cold-blooded
- Most lay eggs
- Moist skin
- Live partly in water

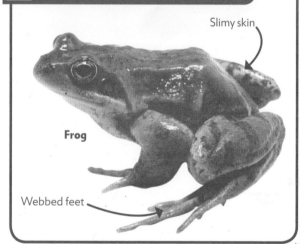

Slimy skin

Frog

Webbed feet

Reptiles

Key features
- Cold-blooded
- Most lay eggs
- Some give birth to live young
- Scaly skin

Scaly skin

Snake

Birds

Key features
- Warm-blooded
- Lay eggs
- Feathered
- Most can fly

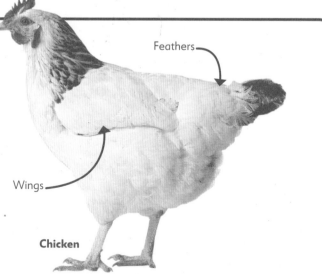

Feathers

Wings

Chicken